ORGANIZATIONAL POVERTY: Valuing Human Capital in Non-Profit Settings

By:

Dr. Lydia Hughes- Evans

Preface

This book has come to life from the 15+ years of experience that I've had working in non-profit agencies and school settings. Large or small, public or private, and regardless of service provision type, I've found that an organizational poverty mindset can subtly engulf an agency, without warning and without mercy. Many agency leaders discern that something is amiss, but are unable to pin-point this elusive and intangible source of organizational distress, let alone determine a plan of action for its eradication. This book gives us a shared language by which to name and thereby control this phenomena, in addition to providing tools to elevate and transform non-profit organizations and staff.

Dedication

I dedicate this book to each non-profit agency that I've come into contact with, past, present, and future.

About the Author

Dr. Lydia Hughes- Evans is Owner & Principal Consultant of Pure Momentum Consulting. Her extensive experience has led her to work with both organizations and individuals in various capacities, including as an organizational consultant, group home administrator, teacher, vocational counselor, trainings facilitator, and tutor. She has exercised her entrepreneurial muscles as owner of Pure Momentum Consulting for the past 11 years. Dr. Lydia received her Bachelors of Arts in English & Psychology from Maryville University, and both her Masters of Education and Doctorate in Organizational Leadership, from Argosy University. Her passion is to provide organizational strategy and design support to non-profits, which seek to promote employee engagement, and propel agency efficiency and effectiveness. Dr. Lydia enjoys reading and traveling in her spare time, and currently resides in the beautiful San Francisco Bay Area of northern California.

Table of Contents

Introduction 9

CHAPTER 1: Organizational Poverty Matrix and Assessment 14

CHAPTER 2: Adaptable Infrastructure 22

CHAPTER 3: Resourcefulness and Collaboration 37

CHAPTER 4: Burnout 43

CHAPTER 5: Staff Development 49

CHAPTER 6: Organizational Sustainability 61

Ending Remarks 72

References 75

Introduction

Non-profit organizations in America are currently facing foundation-altering challenges unlike ever before. Funding constraints, increasing compliance regulations, the speed of technological advancements, and severe staffing shortages threaten to unravel the very fabric of many legacy agencies, as well as newly minted corporations. According to the University of Notre Dame, non-profits nationwide are grappling with the following challenges:

Fiscal Concerns – How do non-profits change pre-existing patterns, and identify new funding sources?

Competition – How do non-profits make themselves stand out? How do they utilize brand recognition to energize and mobilize their supporters?

Effectiveness – How do non-profits measure and promote effectiveness by establishing goals, and how do they keep donors aware of what has been accomplished?

Infrastructure – How does a non-profit utilize its resources to build a solid infrastructure?

Legitimacy – How do non-profits overcome public skepticism and distinguish themselves from organizations that overpromise but under-deliver?

Growth – How do non-profits continue to grow, affect change, and ensure a lasting positive impact? (University of Notre Dame, 2017)

The Organizational Poverty Mindset

In the face of the foregoing concerns, in addition to an increased need for client services, it is not surprising that many agencies have inadvertently developed an *organizational poverty* mindset. Poverty at its core dwells in the realm of *lack*, the belief – and possibly the realistic assessment – that there is not enough of something. This author defines organizational poverty as an inherent sense of lack that pervades an organizational culture: there isn't enough money, there isn't enough staff, there aren't enough clients, there aren't enough resources, etc. Rather than approaching a situation from a place of abundance, agencies that suffer from this malady tend to view the world around them, and their very existence, from a place of "not enough." This collective mindset seeps into the organizational subconscious, paralyzing everyone and everything that enters its vortex. Many non-profits serve vulnerable, traumatized, and disenfranchised individuals, who may also live in a state of socioeconomic and educational poverty. If left untreated, the organizational poverty mindset is very much akin to the beliefs and experiences of impoverished individuals and societies, creating an internal parallel process within the agency similar to that of the clients who receive services.

The Cure

Non-profit leaders engage in a daily balancing act of enthusiastically fulfilling the mission and vision of the agency, while also encouraging and developing its human capital, which is any organization's greatest and most invaluable resource. Without a vibrant and motivated staff, the agency is left with a collection of evidence-based practices, office cubicles, and outdated fax machines. It is the agency staff that will bring life, vitality, and purpose, thereby forwarding and implementing the vision. Having worked in a variety of non-profit settings, for large and small agencies, in different states, and in various roles, this author is confident of this one thing: A non-profit agency without healthy staff is indeed poor. This book offers practical solutions to fiscal, infrastructural, and systemic challenges faced by the modern non-profit, within the framework of valuing human capital. Within these pages lies a roadmap for assessing, developing, and implementing strategies that will shift an organizational mindset from one of poverty and lack, to a perspective of abundance and opportunity.

How to Use this Book

This book is developed to serve as a comprehensive tool for the diagnosis and cure of the organizational poverty mindset. The first chapter of the book presents the Organizational Poverty Matrix developed by the author, along with a subsequent assessment to be completed. When completing the assessment, be honest about the current state of the agency: not where it *could* be, but where it is right now. The assessment consists of 40 questions within four categories, which help to further delineate key organizational components that may need to be shifted to disrupt the poverty mindset.

The score in each of the four categories will give a sense of both agency progress and areas in need of improvement. A score of 70% or below in any category signifies significant underlying concerns that may impede the achievement of the agency vision and mission. Each of the categories directly relates to subsequent chapters within the book. Each chapter is formatted to present an introduction to the topic, related symptomology, prescriptions for a cure, and reflective questions to guide next steps.

Read on…

CHAPTER 1:

Organizational Poverty Matrix and Assessment

Organizations are comprised of numerous moving pieces and parts that, when in relationship, form the macro and micro structures of an agency. The alignment of these parts is critical to produce an efficient and effective operation. The Organizational Poverty Matrix serves as a unit of analysis by which to evaluate the abundance of an agency, in relation to the health of its infrastructure, resources, staff, and legacy. This knowledge is crucial to exposing impoverished beliefs and actions, which stem from a place of lack. The model presents a holistic view of common pitfalls that can plague non-profits. Each category, though significant in its own right, is also part of the larger organizational picture. Decisions and changes made in each category significantly impact the other three corresponding areas.

Organizational Poverty Matrix

Adaptable Infrastructure	Resourcefulness & Collaboration
Staff Engagement	Sustainability

Figure 1

Complete the assessment for each of the following areas: Adaptable Infrastructure, Resourcefulness and Collaboration, Staff Engagement, and Sustainability.

Adaptable Infrastructure

1) Does the internal structure of the organization serve as an effective foundation for the achievement of agency vision, mission, and objectives?
2) Is the organizational culture healthy enough to withstand the ebbs and flows of leadership, fiscal, and regulatory compliance changes?

3) Do the standard operating procedures and other agency policies support the achievement of agency vision, mission, and objectives?

4) Has the agency created, implemented, and evaluated a strategic plan?

5) Do employee job descriptions match their actual day-to-day experiences?

6) Do the job descriptions clearly delineate aligned responsibilities above and below each job role in the agency, thus reducing redundancies and lack of clarity?

7) Is there a systems and work-flow chart that clearly describes the relationship between individual job tasks and departmental/interdepartmental goals?

8) Is there a systems and work-flow chart that clearly describes the relationship between interdepartmental goals, executive leadership tasks, and the achievement of agency goals and objectives?

9) Have functional systems of checks and balances been created to assess decision-making processes and structural gaps or misfits within the agency?

10) Is there a process for incremental assessment and evaluation of the agency's infrastructure and design?

If it is assessed that the organization has answered "No" to 3 or more of the foregoing questions, read Chapter 2: *Adaptive Infrastructure*.

Resourcefulness and Collaboration

1) Is the organization efficiently and effectively utilizing all internal and external resources at its disposal?

2) Are financial resources efficiently assessed, stewarded, and distributed with an eye toward the achievement of the agency vision and mission?

3) Are human capital resources effectively managed, coached, and evaluated throughout all levels within the agency?

4) Are physical resources such as buildings, grounds, and equipment proactively assessed and maintained?

5) Are knowledge management and communication structures effectively facilitated within the organization?

6) Is technological and operational equipment consistently evaluated, maintained, and replaced as needed?

7) Does the agency actively seek opportunities to engage in mutually beneficial strategic collaborative partnerships?

8) Does the agency effectively utilize external resources to support deficits in internal resources?

9) Does the organization maintain a significant level of engagement with the surrounding community, including other non-profit agencies, businesses, faith-based institutions, and advocacy groups?

10) Is there a process for incremental assessment and evaluation of opportunities to increase resourcefulness and collaboration?

If it is assessed that the organization has answered "No" to 3 or more of the foregoing questions, read Chapter 3: *Resourcefulness and Collaboration.*

Staff Engagement

1) Does the agency implement best practices in the on-boarding, training, evaluation and disciplinary functions of staff management?

2) Are there structures set in place to effectively evaluate, address, and prevent workplace stress and staff burnout?

3) Do systems exist to effectively evaluate, address, and mitigate the impact of vicarious trauma?

4) Are all staff encouraged and coached to practice resilience in the workplace?

5) Are all staff placed in positions that maximize their innate skills, talents, and gifts?

6) Does the agency champion the development of employee competence and mastery of job tasks and roles, particularly those of mid-management supervisors?

7) Does the organization promote the intrinsic motivation of all employees?

8) Are consistent opportunities for appreciation, positive recognition, and incentives built into the organizational culture and structure?

9) Does the agency provide ample and relevant staff development and training opportunities, both internal and external, to all staff?

10) Is there a process for incremental assessment and evaluation of staff development, engagement, and retention?

If it is assessed that the organization has answered "No" to 3 or more of the foregoing questions, read Chapter 4: *Burn Out*, and Chapter 5: *Staff Development*.

Sustainability

1) Does the agency actively engage in succession planning for all agency leaders, including the Board of Directors?

2) Does the agency regularly create plans and implement effective strategies for fund development, donor cultivation, and fiscal contingency planning?

3) Does the organization actively engage in board and executive leadership development?

4) Are evaluative processes set in place to prevent the over-extending of job roles and duties for staff?

5) Are effective change management principles practiced throughout the agency?

6) Are relevant bodies of knowledge – organizational history, changes in vision, direction, or strategy – effectively communicated and archived within the agency?

7) Does the agency practice effective brand development and marketing strategies?

8) Does the agency utilize relevant technology to capture compliance, quality assurance, and community impact data?

9) Does the organization have a plan that promotes further engagement with the surrounding community including other non-profit agencies, businesses, faith-based institutions and advocacy groups?

10) Is there a process for incremental assessment and evaluation of agency sustainability and legacy creation?

If it is assessed that the organization has answered "No" to 3 or more of the foregoing questions, read Chapter 6: *Sustainability*.

CHAPTER 2:

Adaptable Infrastructure

Every company has two organizational structures: The formal one is written on the charts; the other is the everyday relationship of the men and women in the organization. Harold Geneen

Introduction

The infrastructure of the organization serves as the skeleton on which the muscles of human capital reside. An unbalanced and disjointed skeleton impedes organizational movement. According to Burton et. al. (2015), agency infrastructure is comprised of structural components such as goals, strategy, and organizational design, and human components such as work processes, people, and incentive mechanisms. It is imperative that non-profit agency leaders consistently evaluate agency infrastructures, as unseen gaps and alignment misfits can perpetuate the perception of organizational poverty. If left undiagnosed, a poor organizational design can cause an agency to operate on only four out of six possible cylinders, causing excessive strain on agency staff and resources. Organizational design, structure, and strategy can be an elusive and complex phenomena to pin down. Although there are numerous factors and methodologies that support adaptable infrastructure, this chapter will focus on the following three tenets: strategy, task design, and people space.

Strategy

Organizational strategy can be described in the following ways: Defender, Reactor, Prospector (Burton et al, 2015). The *defender* **strategy** focuses on maintaining market positioning, as opposed to exploring new opportunities and resources. While defender agencies are efficient at utilizing resources, they are slow to acknowledge or implement change. Threats to the defender strategy include reduction in the demand for products or services, as well as technological advancements. The *reactor* **strategy** is neither efficient nor effective in achieving the mission or vision. Reactor agencies may fail to identify timely opportunities for innovation or industry trends, or may choose to pursue innovation without aligning a strategic focus on the vision and mission of the organization. Problems are seen as surprises and are dealt with in isolation, as opposed to being addressed within the context of the big picture. Threats to the reactor strategy include organizational change, mergers or closure, and industry regulation or deregulation. The ***prospector* strategy** values innovation, but lacks the ability to efficiently utilize its resources. "It searches continually for new market opportunities and experiments regularly with new ideas, new technology, and new processes" (Burton et. al., 2015). While prospecting agencies tend to set the trend within their industry, and weather changes in products and services more gracefully than defender agencies, their service quality and competitive pricing tend to be of lesser importance. Threats to the prospector strategy include new product or service development cycles, as well as compliance regulations. It is obvious that most organizations go through each of these *growth stages* of strategy at various times within the agency life-cycle. The key is to build contingency plans that can mediate the risks associated with each strategy, to promote a balanced and progressive approach towards the agency vision and mission.

Task Design

Task design divides work into sub-tasks, and defines the coordination between sub-tasks, toward the aim of meeting organizational goals. Once again, the *macro* is separated into the *micro*. Task design decisions are typically made in relationship to organizational goals and structure. Burton et. al. (2015) describes four basic task designs: orderly, complicated, fragmented, and knotty. **Orderly task design** organizes work in a way that is highly divisible and highly repetitive, with a top-down process of decision making. This style of task design offers certain advantages: lack of achievement in one department doesn't negatively impact other departments, and the standardization of tasks can yield high efficiency. Disadvantages include a lack of coordination between individuals completing sub-tasks. **Complicated task designs** are not easily divisible, remain repetitive, and require a high degree of coordination. This task design is appropriate for processing high volumes of work. Agency leadership focuses on the coordination of connected processes, as is the norm for many non-profit organizations. Advantages include the ability to individualize products and services, along with the ability to facilitate a high level of information processing. Disadvantage include the potential of a singular task breakdown can negatively impact the entire operation, and the need to devote continuous attention to task coordination. *Fragmented task design* is easily divisible but low on repetitiveness, and requires less coordination then complicated task designs. This can promote sub-task innovation, because sub-units can operate more autonomously. Advantages include a decreased need to focus on coordination from leadership, and more of a focus on obtaining resources to complete sub-tasks. Disadvantages include a decreased standardization of work processes. *Knotty task design* requires low divisibility and repetitiveness. "This approach to task design encourages those responsible for sub-tasks to develop innovative ways to do their work, accommodating the unique demands of each customer, while at the same time those performing sub-tasks must integrate their work with other units of the firm." (Burton et al, 2015) Advantages include opportunities to explore new services or products. Disadvantages include the level of complex challenge for managers who oversee a knotty task design.

One may wonder why the author has spent so much time on this technical section. The type of task design chosen is typically based upon the organizational structure and the types of services rendered by the agency. It is quite possible for an agency to have two or more types of task designs occurring in various parts of the organization simultaneously. For example, an agency that operates group homes for children may choose to enact a complicated task design for administrative functions, while relying more on a knotty task design for direct care staff. Therefore, it is imperative that agency leadership maintain a firm knowledge of staff tasks, employ task designs that promote efficiency within departments, and evaluate whether the end-products enhance the achievement of the agency mission and vision.

People Space

The organization, management, and alignment of human capital resources greatly affect the ability of an organization to achieve its goals. Burton et. al. (2015) shares the following four theories for people space: shop, factory, laboratory, and office. The *shop approach* for people management is common among agencies that have smaller staffs and are low on professionalism, as defined by levels of specialized training and experience. This includes agencies that employ individuals who are only given a few days of training. Staff typically wait to take direction from management, and are not encouraged to develop skills individually, make decisions, or advance changes. Advantages include a reduced need for information-processing and the formation of simple routines. However, the shop approach works poorly when applied to a more expansive staff, or a professionally trained workforce. The *factory approach* employs many people who are low in professionalism. This approach includes simple and repetitive routines, but also involves high coordination of tasks. Individuals with focused skill sets may benefit from this approach, as opposed to individuals with broader professionalization. The *laboratory approach* is well-suited to smaller staffs, with higher professionalization. Work is more autonomous, and managers serve to support the individual. Advantages include a reduced need for work coordination. Potential disadvantages include greater variations in routines and a reduced sense of organizational control. The *office approach* employs many people who are each highly professional, due to extensive education, training, and experience. High-level routines and individual autonomy necessitate more complex information processing and sharing systems, efficient inter-departmental and executive communication, and opportunities for learning and development. Potential disadvantages include an increased demand for coordination and effective supervision.

Evaluating organizational strategy, task design, and people space requires a firm knowledge of organizational vision and goals, infrastructure opportunities and challenges, industry requirements, and the needs of the clients receiving services. There is no one-size-fits-all approach to creating an adaptable infrastructure. The purpose of this introduction is to highlight the wealth of possibilities and options that are available to non-profit leaders when assessing organizational infrastructure. Ultimately, if an organization is failing to experience optimal achievement of agency goals, it is imperative to take a closer look at the internal organization of processes and people.

Symptoms of Non-Adaptable Infrastructure

- Departmental silos
- Excessive internal conflict
- Unclear roles, communication methods, decision and reporting structures, and responsibilities
- Poor workflows and decreased productivity
- High employee turnover
- Misused and under-utilized resources

Prescription

Non-adaptable infrastructure and a poor organizational design stand to exacerbate the organizational poverty mindset, and places an excessive strain on staff. Upon proper evaluation, agencies may discover that what they've "needed all along" is already present, right underneath their nose. Consider the following three recommendations:

Adaptable Infrastructure Model

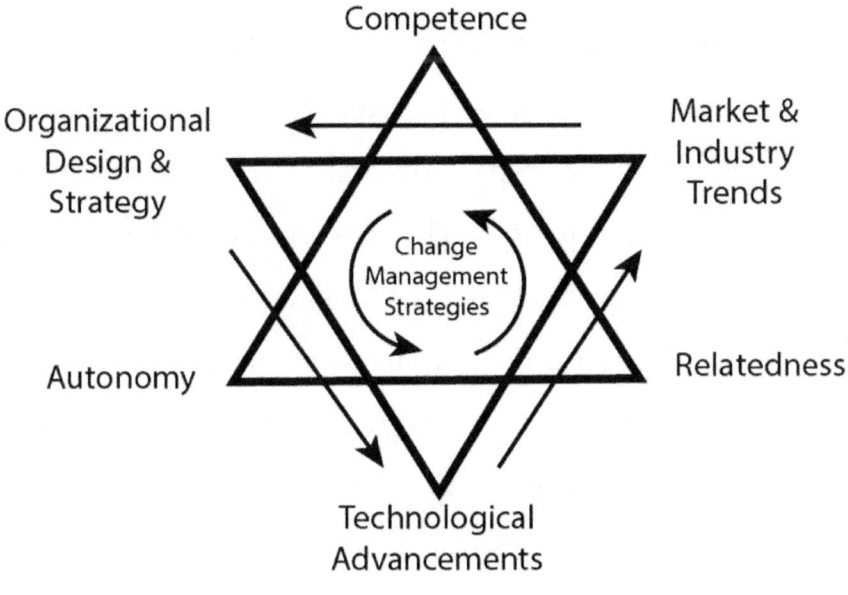

Figure 3

1) **Evaluate, diagnose, and eliminate misfits in organizational design.** If no one has given thought to the design of the agency for the past 20 years, now is the time. Consider conducting an evaluation of the following: goals and scope, strategy, structure, processes and people, coordination, control, and incentives (Burton et. al., 2015). Enlisting the support of an Organizational Consultant will increase the likelihood of a beneficial outside perspective and tailored recommendations for improvement.

2) **Review the Adaptable Infrastructure Model, and create a plan to bring both structural and human capital components into alignment.** The model, consisting of two overlapping triangles, serves to represent the impact of organizational infrastructure upon employees. The first triangle (Competence, Autonomy, and Relatedness) comprises the basic tenets of intrinsic motivation, which is discussed further in Chapter 5: *Staff Development*. This triangle represents the employee. The second triangle (Organizational Design & Strategy, Market & Industry Trends, and Technological Advancements) represents aspects of the agency infrastructure, which impact the day-to-day completion of work tasks. There is a cyclical relationship between Organizational Design & Strategy, Market & Industry Trends, and Technological Advancements. They are both independently ever-changing, as well as simultaneously exercising their impact on one another – and on the employee. Learning organizations effectively implement change-management strategies, which enable leaders to create adaptable

organizational designs, in addition to promoting employee intrinsic motivation, which strengthens employee engagement and commitment. Movement on the structural and human capital fronts is a constant occurrence, and will only increase due to technological advancements, funding constraints, and client need for services.

3) **Implement effective change management strategies.** All of this moving and shifting shakes up the organizational infrastructure, most importantly, for the staff. It is essential that agency leaders are equipped to effectively manage change within their organization, and to support employees during times of transition. An inability to do so will result in both a physical and an emotional loss of an organization's most precious resource: its employees. This author recommends *The Heart of Change*, by John P. Kotter. Kotter's practical and widely utilized eight-step change management model is a great place to start:

    a. **Create a sense of urgency.** Organizational change can be a slow process, particularly for legacy agencies; just getting started can be like pulling teeth.

b. **Build a guiding team.** Effective change requires engagement from all levels within the agency. Include representatives from each department, to be sure that change initiatives are standardized and implemented cohesively throughout the agency.

c. **Create a vision for internal change.** All non-profits have an established vision and mission, which maximizes client and community impact. Staff must see and embrace the vision for internal organizational change as well.

d. **Communicate for buy-in.** Communication flows, throughout all levels of the agency, are key to successful organizational change. Take advantage of this opportunity to equip your interdisciplinary Guiding Team to be change initiators.

e. **Empower action.** Explore individual, departmental, and organizational barriers to change, and develop a plan to mediate them.

f. **Create short-term wins**. Generate small change management wins early, to diffuse cynicism, pessimism, and skepticism. Build momentum!

g. **Don't let up**. Continue to articulate the change vision, and utilize Transformational Leadership strategies (Chapter 5: *Staff Development*) to keep staff encouraged.

h. **Make change stick**. Ensure that staff continue to act in new ways, despite the pull of organizational tradition, by rooting behavior in the reshaped agency culture. Use the employee orientation and training process, coupled with effective performance management and the power of emotion, to establish and integrate new group norms and shared values.

Reflective Next Steps

Which aspects of your organization's infrastructure and design are working well? Which parts need to be fine-tuned? How is the Adaptable Infrastructure Model applicable to your agency? How could your current agency design impact the perception of organizational poverty?

What three things can you do this week to make progress in this area?

CHAPTER 3:

Resourcefulness and Collaboration

*If everyone is moving forward together,
then success takes care of itself.*

Henry Ford

Introduction

Resourcefulness is a significant success indicator for both individuals and organizations. Evaluating, stewarding, sharing, and recycling agency resources can give agency leaders an opportunity to see just how much they have, and how much they may be wasting. Upon these considerations, a sense of abundance begins to develop. Developing strategic collaborative partnerships opens even more doors to an increase in collective organizational prosperity, exponentially expanding client and community impact. To learn more about developing strategic collaborative partnerships, read *Organizational Poverty: Expand Your Impact*, also written by this author. Let's consider the following types of organizational resources:

Financial Resources

The surging retirement numbers among the Baby Boomers, increased financial reporting requirements, changing donor demographics, and tightening industry compliance measures are negatively affecting revenue generation and asset management for many non-profit agencies. Endowments are shrinking, operational costs are increasing, and non-profits are caught in the middle. Many non-profit boards are faced with difficult decisions: provide less services, lay off staff, or close the doors. In these trying times, pro-active fiscal management is essential to the survival of an organization. Contingency planning during the budget preparation process can ensure that there is a Plan B, just in case Plan A doesn't work. Also, looking for areas to "trim the fat" as it were is critical as well. Pay attention to industry trends, and plan for the long-term. Ultimately, passion and enthusiasm alone won't pay the bills.

Human Capital

This author coined the following motto: "Beware of sticking square skills into round roles." Place people in positions that maximize their skills and training, and give them the resources that they need to do their jobs well. Often, the organizational poverty mindset kicks in when there is an unplanned employment vacancy, at either the staff or executive level. Agencies rush to place or promote someone into the position, and hope for the best. Misplaced staffing assignments can result in departmental or organizational stagnation, employee burnout, and will ultimately negatively impact the financial bottom line of the agency. Equip staff with both the technical and leadership training needed to do their jobs effectively. This will create a surge of innovation, commitment, and productivity throughout the agency.

Physical Resources

The routine maintenance of buildings, facilities, and grounds is not the budget line item to cut during a financial crunch. These assets represent years of organizational investments and sacrifices, which should be preserved at all costs, if possible.

Knowledge and Information Management

Eradicate knowledge and information silos or gaps within the organization. As a complex organization with highly motivated, professionally trained staff, information sharing is crucial for success. Examine whether there are any areas in which pertinent knowledge is wrapped up in one person, team, or department, and develop a plan to promote knowledge sharing.

Technological and Operational Equipment

The depth and breadth of technological advancements are here to stay; things will never go back to how they used to be. Emerging technologies such as artificial intelligence and self-driving cars will continue to shape and expand how non-profits operate. Conduct a technology and equipment audit of the organization to determine needs and to recycle unused items.

The underlying imperative here is to thoughtfully consider both agency assets and needs, and create a plan for the fulfillment of those needs. In addition, expand the organizational footprint through the development of strategic collaborative partnerships. Mismanaged and underutilized resources, in addition to operational silos, can perpetuate the experience of organizational poverty.

Symptoms of Underutilized Resources or Resource Gaps

- Increased agency risk and liability
- Lack of innovation and creativity
- Project implementation delays or false starts
- Regression in organizational change management initiatives

Prescription

1) **Create multiple systems to capture the following**, and incorporate the feedback into the organizational design and structure:
    a. Innovative and cost-saving ideas from employees, stakeholders, and vendors

b. Agency resource evaluation assessments and results.

2) **Focus on quality improvement within the agency**. Conduct annual risk assessments, and identify gaps in communications, operations, knowledge management, and service delivery.

Reflective Next Steps

How can your agency manage its resources more effectively? What does your agency need in the following areas?

Financial Resources

Human Capital Resources

Physical Resources

Knowledge Management

Technical and Operational Facets

Which strategic collaborative partnerships could help support your agency in the foregoing areas?

What three things can you do this week to make progress in this area?

CHAPTER 4:

Burnout

Burnout occurs because we're trying to solve the same problem over and over.

Susan Scott

Introduction

Non-profit staff, particularly direct- care human service providers, are subjected to high levels of trauma, anxiety, and stress each day within the context of their work. This phenomenon can place a substantial strain on non-profit organizations. Lambie (2006) described four categories of burnout: a) physical and physiological; b) emotional/psychological; c) interpersonal/clinical; and d) spiritual. "Emotional exhaustion has also been found to spread among providers within organizations, thus further increasing the adverse effects of emotional exhaustion on the organization" (Green, Miller & Aarons, 2013, p. 373).

The combination of burnout, emotional exhaustion, compassion fatigue, and vicarious trauma can lead to high levels of employee turnover within non-profit agencies. Annual turnover rates in agencies providing mental health and social services can exceed 50%, and have been attributed to factors such as high-stress environments, lack of support, and low pay. In organizations providing clinical services, turnover can lead to disruptions in service provision and weaker staff-consumer relationships, thereby negatively affecting the quality and outcomes of services provided by these organizations and their staff (Green et. al., 2013). The bottom line is that non-profit leaders must be able to evaluate and prevent staff burnout before it negatively impacts agency productivity. Staff join non-profit organizations because they are passionate about the vision and mission, and want to be a part of changing the world. They often have no idea of the unique types of stressors facing non-profit workers, until it is too late. Having experienced burnout on a few occasions, this author is acutely aware of the impact it can have on individuals, teams, departments, and agencies. Burnout opens the door for the organizational poverty mindset: "I have nothing left;

therefore we have nothing left to give." Viewing an organization through the eyes of burnout limits possibilities, while placing disproportionate attention on human capital scarcities, and systemic challenges.

Symptoms of Burnout (Carter, 2013)

- Chronic fatigue
- Insomnia
- Forgetfulness; impaired concentration and focus
- Physical symptoms (chest pain, heart palpitations, dizziness, headaches, etc.)
- Increased days off due to illness
- Loss of appetite
- Anxiety, depression, anger, or irritability
- Loss of enjoyment of daily routines
- Detachment and isolation from family, friends, and social circles
- Pessimism and cynicism
- Feelings of apathy and hopelessness
- Lack of productivity and poor job performance.

Prescription

1) **Be sure that staff at all levels within the agency are familiar with, and able to identify, signs of burnout.** Provide staff support through regular discussions and trainings regarding vicarious trauma, compassion fatigue, and workplace stress. Equip staff with the resources necessary to stave off burnout (i.e., confidential access to mental health services, ample time off, etc.). Enlist trained professionals to address chronic and systemic employee burnout within the organization.

2) **Perform a job analysis of direct care positions within the agency.** Tasks that supervisorial staff are unable to complete tend to be pushed down to lower levels of the agency. Direct care staff are on the front lines, and in the immediate line of fire, both from agency mandates and client crises. It is easy to lose perspective, mismanage priorities, and feel isolated in these roles. An annual comprehensive job analysis, including a time-study and a review of job descriptions, will shed some light on the sustainability

of the workload, and offer opportunities to increase staff retention.

3) **Encourage change from the bottom up.** Change is typically implemented from the top-down within organizations. However, direct care staff have candid, first-hand experiences regarding agency strengths, and areas in need of improvement. This information is freely shared between co-workers around the water cooler, but doesn't tend to make it very high in the agency ranks. For this recommendation to work, it is imperative that agency leaders not only collect this information (i.e., suggestion boxes, staff surveys, performance evaluations, informal reviews, etc.), but the organization must intentionally close the feedback loop, by making strategic and tangible changes to its organizational structure, design, and processes. This may be difficult for an organization that is already experiencing a significant bout of employee burnout, but steps can be taken to improve the organizational culture, with the support of trained professionals.

Reflective Next Steps

Is your agency currently experiencing chronic and systemic employee burnout? (A quick way to assess this is to review employee turnover data over the past few months or years.) What are the inherent workplace stressors that exist, in correlation with the type of services that the organization provides? How can you build resilience in the workplace by equipping your staff to successfully manage vicarious trauma, compassion fatigue, and workplace stress?

What three things can you do this week to make progress in this area?

CHAPTER 5:

Staff Development

*The only thing worse than training your employees and having them leave, is **not** training them, and having them stay.*

Henry Ford

Introduction

The Clear Company (2014) recently uncovered some telling statistics from their job satisfaction research:

- 76% of employees want opportunities for career growth
- 25% of employees would be more satisfied at work if they were given the opportunity (and resources) to do what they do best
- 40% of employees who receive poor job training leave their positions within the first year.

Non-profit staff aren't any different. As mentioned in Chapter Four, staff are attracted the vision and mission of the agencies in which they serve, in addition to the compensation or benefits package offered. Staff understand that the likelihood of getting rich while working for a non-profit agency is slim for them. However, as a plethora of job-satisfaction data and the statistics above show, many of the opportunities for non-profit agencies to develop, engage, and retain staff are not directly linked to monetary compensation. The problem is that organizations too often fail to research or pursue these opportunities, thereby short-changing their staff in the area of professional growth. The lack of productivity and performance from underdeveloped staff can also promote a sense of organizational poverty. This section will explore self-efficacy, appreciation and positive recognition, training and development, and intrinsic motivation strategies.

Self-efficacy

Self-efficacy is defined as "the conceptual system of expectations of personal mastery, which affects both initiation and persistence of coping behavior. The strength of people's convictions in their own effectiveness is likely to affect whether they will even try to cope with given situations" (Bandura, 1977, p. 193). Essentially, if individuals believe that they can, they are more likely to try. Non-profit leaders can promote self-efficacy within staff members by equipping them with both the technical, managerial, and resourceful tools necessary to complete their tasks successfully.

Appreciation and Positive Recognition

According to Human Resources Today (2017), approximately 65% of employees reported that they had received minimal positive recognition over the previous 12 months. In the same report, 89% of employers felt that the primary reason for employees leaving a company is to earn more money. This is not so. In fact, most workers who leave their jobs cite lack of appreciation as the catalyst for them to seek other employment opportunities. Consider the following suggestions to foster an organizational culture of appreciation and positive recognition:

1) Establish consistent and measurable criteria for work performance and evaluations.
2) Recognize people from all levels within the agency.
3) Reward employees based on objective accomplishments, as opposed to subjective opinions.
4) Foster a culture of recognition in which informal praise is frequently offered.
5) Align performance benchmarks and standards with the organization's vision, mission, and objectives (Human Resources Today, 2017).

Training and Development

Untrained or improperly trained employees present significant risks and liabilities to an organization, in the form of financial, market-share, and quality-assurance losses. Relevant training and development of staff at all levels are key to the successful performance of an agency. The U.S. Bureau of Labor statistics indicate that companies with fewer than 100 employees provided only 12 minutes of manager training every six months. Organizations with 100-500 employees provided just 6 minutes. A long-term research project conducted by Middlesex University found that, from a study sample of 4,300 employees, 74% felt that they weren't achieving their full potential at work, due to the lack of development opportunities (Shiftlearning.com, 2016). This is unacceptable, particularly in a non-profit agency that provides mental health and social services to clients. Allocate funds during the budgeting process to be intentionally set aside for the quarterly training of direct care staff and middle managers.

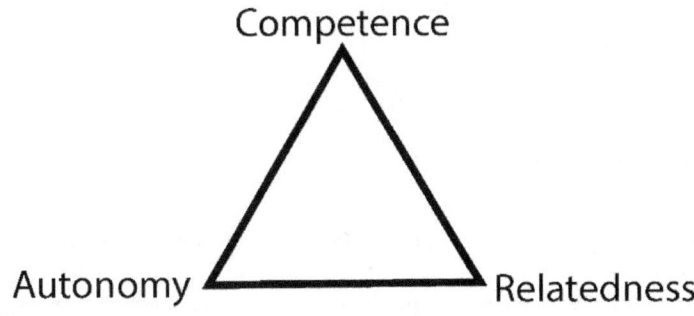

Figure 2

Intrinsic Motivation

In this author's research for her doctoral dissertation titled *Intrinsic Motivation and Counselor Self-Efficacy Perceptions of*

Therapist Interns, a great deal of time was spent exploring the concept of intrinsic motivation. Self-determination theory posits that innate human needs for competence and self-determination propel individuals to seek stimulating challenges, set appropriate goals, and conquer obstacles (Gagne, 2005). Deci (2008) focused on autonomy as an essential concept of self-determination theory and intrinsic motivation literature. **Ryan and Deci** (2000) also added relatedness as another intrinsic need: "Inductively, using the empirical process, we have identified three such needs – the needs for competence, relatedness, and autonomy – that appear essential for facilitating optimal functioning of the natural propensities for growth and integration, as well as for constructive social development and personal well-being" (Ryan & Deci, 2000, p. 68).

Several studies have demonstrated the importance of attending to employee needs in the workplace, particularly autonomy. Baard, Deci, and Ryan (2004) explored the relationship between autonomous managerial support and the satisfaction of employees' intrinsic needs in two empirical studies. Through the lens of self-determination theory, the researchers postulated that intrinsic need satisfaction would predict both performance ratings and the psychological well-being of employees. In the pilot study, 59 employees from a major U.S. bank completed four questionnaires, including the General Causality Orientations Scale; the Problems at Work questionnaire; the General Health Questionnaire; and a 23-question researcher-created questionnaire, designed to assess the satisfaction of intrinsic needs of autonomy, competence, and relatedness. Lastly, participants were requested to provide their most recent performance evaluation. The researchers found that work performance indeed correlated with intrinsic need satisfaction, meaning that individuals who perceived that their intrinsic needs were being met were rated by managers as performing better. In the primary study, 528 study participants completed the General Causality Orientations Scale, the Work Climate Questionnaire, and the Vitality Questionnaire. Again, participants were asked to provide their most recent performance evaluations. The second study found that work performance correlated significantly with intrinsic need satisfaction overall, and with the satisfaction of the independent intrinsic needs of autonomy, competence, and relatedness. Baard et. al. (2004) concluded that the self-determination theory of motivation is relevant and applicable to the workplace.

Symptoms of Staff Development Gaps

- Lack of self-efficacy
- Disengagement with the agency vision or mission
- Apathy
- Decreased productivity and performance
- Increased disciplinary actions
- Increased turnover
- Decreased job satisfaction
- Noncompliance
- Increased organizational mistrust

Prescription

1) **Implement Transformational Leadership strategies.** Transformational leadership is comprised of individualized consideration, intellectual stimulation, inspirational motivation, and idealized influence (Green et. al., 2013) and may provide a way

to increase intrinsic motivation and to meet innate psychological needs in the workplace (Gagne & Deci, 2005; Nanthu, 2013). Non-profit agency supervisors and leaders can exhibit *individualized consideration* by seeking to meet the physical and psychological needs of staff. This can include providing differentiated supervision strategies based on individual needs, offering staff snacks, and providing opportunities for retreats and self-care, as well as promoting the value of a healthy work/life balance within the organizational culture. Agency leaders can provide *intellectual stimulation* for employees by facilitating creativity and innovative thought. Staff could be involved in the development of motivational organizational strategies, incentives to improve employee productivity, and overall organizational performance. This could include conducting a "Strengths, Weaknesses, Opportunities, and Threats" (SWOT) analysis of individual departments and the organization as a whole, as a barometer of employee motivation. *Inspirational motivation* entails developing and implementing a departmental and agency-wide vision. Leaders can engage staff at various levels in the development of organizational missions, visions, values, and operational strategies. An example of this would be the development of a departmental/organizational workplace creed, which is compiled from employee input regarding the optimal functioning of their workplace. Lastly, *idealized influence* is the modeling of expected and acceptable workplace behaviors. Non-profit leaders can provide idealized influence by first determining the core tenets of the agency (i.e., a healthy work-life balance, integrity, effective communication, achievement, or organizational commitment). Once the core tenets have been identified, leaders can exemplify and share these values with staff, and can promote the appreciation and recognition of workers who demonstrate the desired tendencies in the workplace.

2) **Develop and budget for an agency-wide training and development program.**
   a. Determine your training needs by reviewing relevant documents and data points such as agency goals, job descriptions, pertinent compliance regulations, and legal obligations.
   b. Determine who needs to be trained based on organizational goals, job roles and

responsibilities, performance evaluation results, and employee input.
c. Apply the four elements of adult learning:
   i. Intrinsic motivation
   ii. Positive reinforcement of the learning process
   iii. Retention through practice of learned skills
   iv. Transference to apply the learned concepts directly to the workplace.
d. Create an agency training plan.
   i. Determine organizational goals and measurable learning outcomes for each training module.
   ii. List who needs to be trained, within each topic area.
   iii. Create a master training calendar for your agency.
   iv. Integrate a diverse variety of training methods, materials, and training pace to meet the needs of most visual, auditory, and kinesthetic adult learners (Training Today, 2017).

3) **Promote the intrinsic motivation of staff within all levels of the organization.** Csikszentmihalyi's (1975; cited in Smith, 2005) Flow Theory postulated that *flow experiences*, periods of intense involvement in activities that are challenging but not overwhelming, help facilitate intrinsic motivation. To effectively facilitate the development of intrinsic motivation, the task must: (a) meet the individual's skill level; and (b) offer opportunities for complete immersion and focus.

Reflective Next Steps

What is the present state of staff training and development in your agency? What opportunities exist to promote the intrinsic motivation of agency employees? What impact would an intentional focus on appreciation and positive recognition have on the agency?

What three things can you do this week to make progress in this area?

CHAPTER 6:

Organizational Sustainability

I'm here to build something for the long-term.
Anything else is a distraction.

Mark Zuckerberg

Introduction

Non-profit organizations provide positive, meaningful services to the clients and communities that they serve. Agencies that focus on sustainability and legacy planning are better equipped to weather the storms of financial, resource, and staffing challenges. Engaging in proactive, future-focused decision-making is imperative for both legacy agencies and newly minted non-profits. Organizations that fail to plan ahead are unprepared for the unexpected. Consider the following:

Over-extending Staff

The creation of sustainable job roles is essential for the longevity of staff. Many non-profit employees tend to "wear many hats," which seems almost super-human at times, but can also serve as an harbinger of future burnout, exhaustion, and turnover. Audit job descriptions and roles consistently, to ensure that tasks and responsibilities are fairly distributed throughout the agency. If there is a position that appears to be carrying too much, break the tasks down into sub-tasks and delegate those tasks more equitably throughout the department. Organizational cultures that value staff for "coming in early and leaving late," while never really completing or mastering their job tasks, will inadvertently serve as a revolving door for employees. At its worst, high turnover negatively impacts high-quality client service provision.

Organizational Shared History

Most legacy agencies that has been around for 10 or more years have inevitably survived multiple threats to its existence, while continuing to provide relevant, life-changing services to clients. The organization has more than likely changed locations or built new buildings, added innovative service offerings, made substantial improvements through capital campaigns, and weathered numerous economic challenges. It is important to capture, share, and archive these agency achievements, as they serve as the collective history of the organization. It is nearly impossible to know where the agency is headed if there is no knowledge of where it has been. Keep track of change initiatives that have worked, as well as those that didn't. Recognize and honor legacy and major gift donors and their families, along with committed volunteers, past and present. Archive photos and other visuals that represent agency growth spurts and milestones, and share these historical events with present-day staff.

Brand Development and Community Involvement

Don't be afraid to brag! Non-profit leaders tend to shy away from the limelight as they focus on balancing high-quality service provision and operational challenges. However, in this age of social media and visual storytelling, amassing, highlighting, and sharing client and community impact outcomes are essential to the sustainability of the agency. The surrounding community must know that the agency exists, must be aware of the work that it conducts, and must be encouraged to engage in sustaining its longevity. Create a plan that facilitates the building of strategic collaborative partnerships with other non-profit agencies, local businesses, faith-based institutions, and advocacy groups. Pro-actively strive to get the word out by highlighting the strengths and positive impact of the agency. Consider partnering with a marketing firm or with regional media outlets for support in this endeavor.

Symptoms of a Failure to Plan for the Future

- A constant state of organizational crisis
- Reactive, short-sighted decision-making
- Focus on putting out short-term fires, which creates long-term catastrophes
- Organizational stagnation and lack of agility
- Poor or nonexistent community involvement
- Decreased ability to build capacity

Prescription

1) **Create, implement, and evaluate the strategic plan.** Strategic plans assist an agency by serving as a roadmap to, and through, the future. Consider the following strategic planning phases (OnStrategyhq.com):

    a) Determine position.

        i. Decide which strategic issues to address in the plan. Keep it simple, so that the plan can be effectively implemented.

        ii. Conduct a Strengths, Weaknesses, Opportunities and Threats (SWOT) analysis for market and industry data.

        iii. Gather client satisfaction insights and potential future-driven needs.

        iv. Gather employee input (SWOT).

        v. Synthesize all of the research into a summative SWOT.

    b) Develop Strategy

        i. Define the organization's mission and core purpose.

        ii. Identify agency values and core beliefs.

- iii. Create a vision for internal success. How will the organization look, feel, and operate in the next 5 years?
- iv. Delineate the competitive marketplace advantage of the agency.
- v. Decide what it will take to achieve agency-wide success of the strategic plan.
- vi. Choose 6 or fewer long-term objectives, using a 3-year framework for achievement.
- vii. Create a 3-year financial projection model.

c) Build the Plan.
- i. Analyze SWOT data to set priorities.
- ii. Choose short and mid-term organizational SMART objectives (Specific, Measurable, Attainable, Realistic and Timely).
- iii. Identify Key Performance Indicators (KPI) to track progress.

iv. Divide organizational goals into departmental goals to be achieved over the next 12 months.

v. Align departmental goals with individualized roles and tasks. See Chapter 2 Adaptable Infrastructure for more support in this area.

vi. Create a one-year budget in alignment with the objectives of the strategic plan.

d) Manage performance.

i. Communicate the vision, mission, and strategy to the entire organization.

ii. Create a calendar and establish a schedule for progress reviews.

iii. Leverage the agency's human capital, training, and operational resources towards the achievement of strategic planning goals.

iv. Adapt quarterly progress reviews of the plan, and implement modifications as necessary.

v. Update the strategic plan annually, and prepare for the next year.

2) **Practice succession planning.** Wilson (2015) defines succession planning as "any effort designed to ensure the continued effective performance of an organization, division, department, or work group by making provisions for the development, replacement, and strategic application of key people over time." Consider the following strategies:

   a) Establish measurable goals, aligned with the organization's strategic goals, to guide the succession planning process.

   b) Create or revise current job descriptions to reflect current work flows and task designs.

   c) Create competency models based on the levels of the organizational chart. Examine objective performance measurements, and align models with organizational goals.

   d) Carefully define roles played by each key internal stakeholder group: Board, Executive Director or CEO, Senior Directors or

Executives, Middle Managers, Supervisors, and Direct Care Staff.

e) Establish staff talent pools based on the strengths and needs of the organization.

f) Take inventory of human capital resources. Acknowledge both individual strengths and areas in need of improvement.

g) Evaluate the succession planning process annually; compare process and results against succession planning goals; recalibrate the plan based on changing market, industry, and organizational priorities.

3) **Create an organizational dashboard that guides board and executive development.** Consistent and effective board development and training is the first line of defense for organizational sustainability. Chait et. al. (1996) propose the following questions to serve as a guide to identify potential executive training and support opportunities:

a) What is our overall financial performance? Is our revenue structure balanced? Are we deploying our funds appropriately and according to the approved budget?

b) What is the status of key financial ratios (i.e., current assets to liabilities, fixed assets to long-term debt)?

c) How well are we using and managing our resources?

d) Are we in compliance with applicable laws, regulations, and contracts?

e) Are our programs and services achieving expected outcomes?

f) What is the level of current and past client satisfaction?

g) Are we attracting and retaining skilled, dedicated paid staff and volunteers?

h) Is this organization performing at its best?

Reflective Next Steps

What plans are set in place to articulate, evaluate, and preserve the legacy of your organization? How does the agency legacy impact staff, stakeholders, and the community at large? What changes need to be made today to ensure a bright and sustainable organizational future?

What three things can you do this week to make progress in this area?

Ending Remarks

Everyone who has ever done anything significant first found themselves in a place where the status quo was no longer enough.

TemitOpe Ibrahim

This book has explored the impact of perceived organizational poverty through the broad and overlapping lenses of adaptable infrastructure, resourcefulness and collaboration, staff engagement, and organizational sustainability. In addition, the author examined both the interrelatedness and impact of the Organizational Poverty Matrix upon non-profit staff. The purpose of this book is to serve as both an evaluative assessment tool to improve agency efficiency and effectiveness, and a practical guide to making necessary – and successful – adjustments along the way.

Organizational Poverty Spectrum

Organizational Poverty	Functioning	Organizational Abundance
Un-engaged or entrenched Board of Directors	Semi-engaged Board of Directors	Fully engaged Board of Directors
Pervasive lack of a clear vision, mission, or organizational direction = organiizational stagnation or reversal	Partially communicated vision, mission, and organizational direction = partial achievement of agency goals	Clearly communicated vision, mission, and organizational direction = organizational progress
Inefficient systems, workflows, and procedures	Partially efficient systems, workflows, and procedures	Efficient and innovative systems, workflows, and procedures
Poor stewardship of monetary, human capital and collaborative resources	Partially efficient stewardship of monetary, human capital, and collaborative resources	Efficient steardship of monetary, human capital, and collaborative resources
High levels of turn-over within the agency, and an inert organizational culture	Partially engaged staff in various levels of the agency	Fully engaged staff throughout all levels of the agency
Agency is currently operating in crisis mode, struggling to keep it's doors open, and it's future is uncertain	There is a desire to sustain the agency legacy, but few plans have been created or implemented	Clear strategies are designed or implemented to promote an impacftful agency legacy

Figure 4

The bottom line is that agencies with impoverished mindsets fail to recognize and utilize the opportunities and resources at their disposal. Non-profit staff who work in the midst of organizational poverty experience an additional, often intangible strain on their psychological well-being and job performance. It is imperative that agencies that have been hindered by a pervasive impoverished mindset take

immediate action to cultivate an organic shift in the organizational culture. The goal is to implement research-based best practices, which support the following:

1) Bring the organizational vision, mission, design, operational structure, and human capital resources into alignment.
2) Implement lasting and effective agency-wide change-management strategies.
3) Convert the organizational poverty mindset into a fresh, opportunity-driven perspective of organizational abundance.

Only then can the non-profit organization completely and effectively fulfill its primary mission: to make our world a better place for everyone. I would love to hear how you've used Systems & Processes to value your staff and volunteers! Visit our website at: www.puremomentumconsulting.com.

In Abundance,

Dr. Lydia

References

Bandura, A. (1977). Self-efficacy: Toward a unifying theory of behavioral change. *Psychological Review (84)2*, 191-215

Baard, P; Deci, E; and Ryan, R. (2004). Intrinsic need satisfaction: A motivational basis of performance and well-being in two work settings. *Journal of Applied Social Psychology (34)10*, 2045-2068

Burton, R. et.al. (2015). *Organizational Design: A Step by Step Approach.* United Kingdom: Cambridge University Press

Carter, S. (2013). The Tell Tale Signs of Burnout… Do You Have Them? https://www.psychologytoday.com/blog/high-octane-women/201311/the-tell-tale-signs-burnout-do-you-have-them. Retrieved: October 11, 2017

Chait, R. et.al. (1996). *Improving the Performance of Governing Boards.* Phoenix, AZ: Oryx Press

Clear Company. (2014). 5 Surprising Employee Development Statistics You Don't Know.

https://blog.clearcompany.com/5-surprising-employee-development-statistics-you-dont-know. Retrieved: October 8, 2017

Deci, E. (2008). Facilitating optimal motivation and psychological well-being across life's domains. *Canadian Psychology (49)*1, 14-23

Gagne, M. (2005). Self-determination theory and work motivation. *Journal of Organizational Behavior (26)*4, 331-362

Gagne, M.; Deci, E. (2005). Self-determination theory and work motivation. *Journal of Organizational Behavior (26)*1, 331-362

Green, A.; Miller, E.; and Aarons, G. (2013). Transformational leadership moderates the relationship between emotional exhaustion and turnover intention among community mental health providers. *Community Mental Health Journal (49)*1, 373-379

Human Resources Today.com (2017). 12 Powerful Tips to Build an Employee Recognition Culture. http://www.humanresourcestoday.com/2017/employee-recognition/?open-article-id=6265947&article-

title=12-powerful-tips-to-build-an-employee-recognition-culture&blog-domain=employeeconnect.com&blog-title=employeeconnect. Retrieved: October 6, 2017

Kotter, J. (2002). *The Heart of Change*. Boston, MA: Harvard Business School Press

Lambie, G. (2006). Burnout prevention: A Humanistic perspective and structured group supervision activity. *Journal of Humanistic Counseling, Education and Development (45)*1, 32-44

Nanthu, Y. (2013). Intrinsic motivation: How can it play a pivotal role in changing clinician behavior. *Journal of Health Organization and Management (27)*2, 266- 272

OnStrategyhq.com (2017). Essentials Guide to Strategic Planning. https://onstrategyhq.com/resources/strategic-planning-process-basics/. Retrieved: October 10, 2017

Ryan, R.; Deci, E. (2000). Self-determination theory and the facilitation of intrinsic motivation, social development and well-being. *American Psychologist (55)*1, 68-78

Shiftelearning.com (2016). 10 Statistics on Corporate Training and What They Mean for Your Companys Future. https://www.shiftelearning.com/blog/statistics-on-corporate-training-and-what-they-mean-for-your-companys-future. Retrieved: November 1, 2017

Smith, J. (2005). Flow theory and GIS: Is there a connection for learning ? *International Research in Geographical & Environmental Education (14)*3, 223-230

TrainingToday.com (2017). Creating a Custom Training Plan for Your Organization. http://trainingtoday.blr.com/article/creating-a-custom-training-plan/. Retrieved: November 15, 2017

Wilson, T. (2015). 8 Steps for Effective Succession Planning. https://www.halogensoftware.com/blog/8-steps-for-effective-succession-planning. Retrieved: October 17, 2017

University of Notre Dame. (2017) Six Challenges Facing the Non- Profit Sector. https://www.notredameonline.com/resources/nonprofit-leadership/six-challenges-facing-the-nonprofit-sector/#.WmK4MrCIbos. Retrieved: October 10, 2017